Jenny Mosley's Top Tips for

Calmer Classrooms

Positive Press

Published in 2014 by:
Positive Press Ltd
28A Gloucester Road
Trowbridge
Wiltshire BA14 0AA

Telephone: 01225 719204
Fax: 01225 712187
E-mail: positivepress@jennymosley.co.uk
Website: www.circle-time.co.uk

Printed 2014
ISBN: 978-1-904866-63-3

Printed in the UK by www.heronpress.co.uk

Contents

Introduction

Research tells us the best learning happens in classrooms where the challenge is high but the sense of 'threat' is low. Children need to feel emotionally safe. What makes a classroom feel safe? Children need to know that they will be treated fairly. They need to feel supported. They need to be untroubled. In other words, children learn best in a classroom that is calm!

This little book is a distillation of Jenny's top tips for a calm, hardworking and successful classroom. These include ways in which you can embed calmness into the structure of your classroom routines and how to relax and refresh children when the going gets tough and they become restless. The book will show you practical approaches to learning that will help your children to achieve through giving them opportunities to relax, breathe and feel calm.

Be the calm person you want to see

As Gandhi said, 'be the change that you want to see'. You want a calm classroom so you need to find calm within yourself. When the leader is calm then everyone around them feels secure and comfortable. Unfortunately anxiety and anger are 'catching' too, so it is crucial that you create the right atmosphere. You are the leader and everyone wants to be led by someone who projects calm, assertive energy.

Choose a 'guide'

The imagination is a powerful tool. Use it to help you become a calm, assertive leader. Think of someone who inspires you. This person can be real or imagined. Use them as your guide. Think about how they move and speak – how they communicate calm assertiveness. Study them, copy them and become like them. Assertive calmness can be learned, and then you can teach this essential way of being to the people and children you work with.

Body language

Stand straight and relaxed. Keep your head up. Keep your gaze steady. Keep your movements as controlled and deliberate as possible. Relax your face, smile whenever you can to relax others.

Speak calmly and assertively

Speak slowly and clearly and think about what you need to say. Expect to be heard and you will be. Pause a little so that your listeners have time to absorb what you are saying. Lower your voice when you need to convey something important – soft voices are more powerful because children have to concentrate to hear.

Breathe

Steady breathing is the essence of being calm. Try this breathing exercise if you feel yourself becoming tense: *focus your attention on something in front of you. Take a very deep breath and hold it for a moment. Purse your lips so that they are very tight and slowly send the air out in a little hissing stream that makes a quiet 'sssss' sound.*

When you have a moment and are sitting down – practice deeper breathing. Get yourself comfortably settled in the chair with your back supported and your feet slightly apart. Put your hand on your stomach and close your eyes. Close your mouth and slowly breathe in through your nostrils to a count of three, so you push your hand out with your stomach. Then breathe out through your mouth to the same count of three, so that your hand goes in (press it down slightly more firmly to expel the last bit of stale air). This is a great technique to practice and it's a wonderful one to teach to children who need to learn anger management.

Golden Moments

Calmness is a beautiful thing that needs to be fed and sustained. Nurture yourself with Golden Moments. This means mindfully doing things that refuel your spirit and senses and can include anything that makes you feel calm, relaxed and joyful. Take a few minutes 'out' during your busy day. Stand outside with a cup of tea, feel the heat of the cup, feel the wind/sun on your face, breathe calmly and be aware of the stillness. Make sure that you give yourself plenty of these moments throughout the day. They don't need to take long, but they are essential.

The Calming Environment

Imagine a peaceful place. Hold that image in your mind. Think about the qualities that make it so serene. Consider how you could recreate those qualities in your working environment.

Tidy classroom – tidy minds

If you eliminate clutter from your classroom, you eliminate confusion. Clearing out creates space and space is always peaceful. Make sure your working space is clean and organised and everyone knows where to find the things they need.

Tidiness creates respect

A tidy classroom teaches respect for learning, respect for property and respect for one another. It shows that you value the children enough to give them an environment that makes it easier to achieve excellence. Have a 'pet' puppet that lives in the classroom that loves tidiness (the puppet is the one that nags them to put things away, not you).

Labelling

Children need to know where to find the things they need. Clear labelling helps them to find things without becoming anxious and flustered. Once you have designated a place for each item they need, that place needs to remain constant – don't move things around. Give children the much loved jobs of being 'book minders', wiping the board monitor, etc.

Quiet Zone

Every environment needs a quiet space that everyone can use when they need a little more calm; a refuge that can be accessed whenever it is needed. It should be comfortable and sheltered. How about velvet cushions, some water and a sand timer for how long they've earned to 'cool off'?

Seating arrangements

Make sure that all the children can see you and the board easily. If seats are facing away from you, ask the children to stand up and change their seats around when necessary. Arrange your classroom to optimise flexibility and easy movement between groups. Ensure that you have a focal area to which you always go when you need to speak to the whole class – children need consistency.

Posters

Wall posters that remind children of their responsibility to help keep the classroom a calm environment are very useful because they can be quietly pointed at. Put them in strategic places on your walls and ensure that they are explained and discussed regularly. Try to ensure that they are at eye level and change them when you can.

Calming Golden Rules

Being calm means being peaceful and quiet. It is how we feel when we are without anxiety. Calmness thrives when positive values are consistently promoted and every child is able to concentrate on learning because they feel safe, secure and valued. We establish this sense of order through the Golden Rules.

There are six Golden Rules:

1. We are gentle … We don't hurt others.
2. We are honest … We don't cover up the truth.
3. We listen … We don't interrupt.
4. We are kind and helpful … We don't hurt anybody's feelings.
5. We look after property … we don't damage things.
6. We work hard … We don't waste time.

In order to establish the Golden Rules in your classroom we suggest that you:

- Introduce the Golden Rules through Circle Time and make sure that the children have time to discuss them fully.

- Make the Golden Rules visual. Use posters and photographs so that children can see the rules in action.

- Reinforce the Golden Rules with praise, encouragement and joy.

- Pair children up so that struggling children can be helped by a more reliable peer. Remember to thank these children!

- Use cards that reinforce the Golden Rules quietly and effectively. For example, 'Peace Cards', showing a rainbow, which can be placed near to children who are keeping the rules well. There are also 'Warning Cards', which are placed near children who are losing focus. A second transgression could lead to losing Golden Time. (See 'Golden Time' p.9)

- Give your children as many positive affirmations as you can. These could include statements. For instance, 'I am successful and know how to work hard', 'I will succeed today', 'We are always kind' and 'We always help each other'.

- Have a 'Jar of Good Choices'. All you need is a glass jar and some big golden marbles. Whenever you or a child notices that they are abiding by a particular golden rule (your target for the day) they will receive a golden marble. Every time they are nominated you say 'Good choice – you have kept the Golden Rule of listening'. Dramatically put it in the jar with all the children listening, so it makes a 'kerchink' sound which you call the 'sound of a good choice'! When the jar is full the whole class has a short treat.

- Enlist the help of parents and carers. Explain the Golden Rules to all the adults who care for each child. Send home letters and certificates. Research has shown that plentiful praise and positive feedback makes children feel secure and calm. Criticism just makes them anxious.

Golden Time

Golden Time is a whole school incentives and consequences system (see resources page for 'Better Behaviour Through Circle Time' book). It is a celebration of success and acknowledgement of respect for all the children who always keep the Golden Rules.

- Golden Time is timetabled into the school week as part of the curriculum for teaching moral values. This is usually a weekly event, but can be daily for some children.
- Joining in Golden Time is a reward for children who have kept the Golden Rules. Conversely, it is used as a sanction for children who have not kept the rules.
- Children earn the right to enjoy Golden Time. Their progress is made visual using three large cut-outs: a large bright yellow sun, a sun partly obscured by cloud and a grey cloud. Each child has a peg with their name on it which is pegged on the sun. It is placed on the sun/cloud as a warning. If the warning is not heeded, the peg is placed on the grey cloud and the right to one minute of Golden Time is lost.
- When Golden Time takes place, any child with a grey peg on a cloud sits away from the activity area while looking at a sand timer.
- Adults and children work together to choose activities for Golden Time. Any safe enjoyable activity can be included: games, music, dancing, painting, helping in the office, picnic, jigsaws, quiet time etc.
- Teachers make laminated, reusable activities lists. Children can sign up for particular activities on Monday morning and look forward to them all week.
- You talk to your class regularly to make sure they know that you believe they are all capable of keeping the Golden Rules and earning some Golden Time fun.
- You make sure children understand the concept of losing Golden Time and how to gain it back. They need to know that this system happens every day in a firm but fair way. .
- You keep Golden Time fresh and exciting with fundraising to buy new equipment, collect old birthday/Christmas cards for 'Cut and stick' and involve parents and visitors.
- Have a special Golden Time trolley with games and activities that can be taken from room to room.

Calming rituals

A calm classroom has an ethos in which children feel valued and secure. One way to create this sense of calm safety is to establish positive classroom rituals. Simple, predictable, positive rituals reduce learner stress and support children through the rigours of each hardworking day.

Be welcoming!

Be at the door to greet students every time they come into your classroom – morning, afternoon and after playtime. Stand straight, be assertively calm and, most importantly, be welcoming and positive. You won't always have time to speak to each child, but keep a mental note of who you have smiled at and talked to so that, over time, you have been seen to be fair. Fairness is a very important concept for children and perceived unfairness can get in the way of all your efforts to achieve a calm classroom.

Settle everyone in with positive relaxation techniques.

Bring your students together at the start of each lesson with quick team building exercises like these:

- *Hands up everyone who's ready to learn something interesting today.*
- *Give me a wave and a smile to show that you're ready for the lesson.*
- *Take a deep breath, hold it for a moment. When you are ready to learn let it out.*
- *Let's clap our favourite song together.*

Preview

Tell the children what they will have achieved by the end of the lesson. Let them watch you write the key words on the white board. Let them repeat this preview to a partner.

Closing rituals

The closing phase of every lesson needs to ensure that children leave the classroom feeling calm and positive. Closing rituals enable everyone to make a smooth transition to the next part of the day. They need to provide appropriate transition activity.

Here are some useful closing rituals:

Breathing exercises

Ask the children to sit still and quietly and let their breathing become steady and slow. Ask them to sit quietly for a few minutes before softly telling them to prepare for the next activity.

Quiet reflection

Ask the children to sit with straight backs, hands resting gently in their laps. Tell them to close their eyes and think about their breathing. Tell them to breathe in a feeling of happiness and calm and, as they breathe out, to let go of any worries or unhappy thoughts. Next, ask them to think about themselves enjoying a lovely warm summer day, doing things that they really enjoy. Finally, they can open their eyes and become aware of the room and the present moment.

Positive feedback

Stand at the door as the children leave and give positive feedback to as many children as you can.

When they are restless

Sometimes the whole class can seem unsettled. Don't battle on regardless. Take a few minutes out to calm and refocus the children with a short activity.

The hand up approach to gaining quiet

The hand up approach to silence is a wonderfully calm way to gain children's attention. Simply hold your arm up very straight and high. Say NOTHING. Stand very still and wait. Children must respond by putting up their hand and silently touching the shoulder of others who are talking and who then put their hand up. Bring your hand down and say 'Thank you'. Sometimes you can hold a closed hand up with a smiley-face sticker inside it, or a 'Golden *good choice* marble' and give this to the first child to respond, and watch the ripple of attention!

Drum roll technique

Quietly but firmly call for a 'drum roll'. The children need to put their hands flat on their knees and gently tap them until you stop the movement by holding your hands out in front of you and then lowering them decisively.

Breathing exercises

Guide the children in a breathing exercise. Tell everyone to sit still and look at you. Ask them to inhale for the count of four, and then exhale for a count of seven. Repeat a few times.

Games

Play a quick game to pull everyone together. Try 'I-Spy' or 'Simon Says', in which you give simple physical instructions like, 'Put your hands on your head', 'Wiggle your nose'.

Mindful moments

Call the children together for a 'mindful moment'. Ask them to look out of the window at an interesting cloud; share a particularly good piece of writing with them or spend a few moments in silence listening to the sounds of the world around them.

Energising

If they need energising, try a short coordination exercise such as a clapping game with a song. Or, put one hand on your nose and the other on the ear opposite to it, then swap hands so the other hand is on your nose etc.

Re-focusing

Re-establish concentration and quick thinking with games that require attention. For example; explain that when you touch your elbow, the children must wave their arms; when you touch your nose they must wiggle their fingers and when you fold your arms they must say 'Oooh'. The children must react correctly to the visual cues and watch carefully. This switches on their concentration

Improve listening skills

Tune up their listening skills with games like 'On Cue'. You give them a key word like 'yellow'. Every time you say this word, they must clap their hands. Make up a story about nothing in particular. Use the word 'yellow' to trigger the desired response.

One minute's peace

When you feel your class is getting too noisy and you need to quieten them, clap your hands and call out, 'One minute's peace'. The children must stop what they are doing and stand up. If you have a wall clock you can train them to turn to face it so that they can watch the second hand.

Calming games

Interactive calming activities promote friendliness and are useful team building tools. Children learn that they can relieve tension as a group and are refreshed by games that promote friendliness and mutual support.

Try these games to help restore calm in your class:

Pass a smile

Smile at one of your children, who should then pass the smile on to another child and so on until everyone in the class has joined in.

Heads up, thumbs down

Choose three or four players to wait at the front of the room. Call out, 'Heads down, thumbs up'. The seated children then put their heads down, close their eyes and put their fists on their ears with the thumbs sticking up. The standing children walk very quickly round the room and choose one person each by gently gripping their thumbs. When a child is touched in this way, they must fold their thumbs into their fists to indicate that they have been chosen. The walkers then return to the front of the room. The players who were touched must try to guess which of the walkers has chosen them. Children who have guessed correctly come to the front and become walkers. The game is played in complete silence and the seated children have an opportunity to relax and relieve tension whilst enjoying an interactive game.

Sleeping Lions

Ask the children to lie down on the floor and pretend to be asleep, keeping themselves as still and as silent as possible. The object of the game is to be the last one to move or to 'wake up'. The leaders should make the job more difficult by creeping between the 'sleeping lions' and making funny comments, or suggesting that children have moved when they have in fact remained still.

Statues (also known as the freezing game)

The children stand as far away from you as possible while you stand facing the wall. The object of the game is for one child to reach your wall without being seen to move. The children need to concentrate and 'freeze' or become a statue when they suspect you'll turn and catch them moving. After several seconds of facing the wall, turn around. Move slowly to keep things calm and, gently tap any child who fidgets. The caught child must calmly return to the starting position.

Simon Says

This game can be very calming if you use calm commands such as, 'Simon says stretch, yawn and breathe' – 'breathe deeply and hold your breath for 5 seconds'.

Ice Age

Ask everyone to stand in a circle. Tell the children that the Ice Age has begun and they are frozen solid and cannot move. Name one part of the body and announce that this is thawing out and can move. Start with fingers and toes and move up the limbs and then slowly move over the rest of the body a little bit at a time. Slowly, their whole body will be 'thawed out' and they will feel quiet and relaxed all over.

Relaxation Techniques

By teaching relaxation techniques you are helping children to lean how to control their anxieties independently and also makes them better learners. The following techniques have proved useful in promoting relaxation in the classroom.

Elephant circles

Put your head on one shoulder and extend your arm so that you are pointing at the children. Draw a circle in the air with your extended hand. The children copy and point back at you. Then tilt your head the other way and, using the other arm, point again. Stretching the neck in this way greatly relieves tension.

Blowing up balloons

Pretend to pull a balloon out of your pocket and encourage the children to do the same. Cup your hands together and hold them in front of your mouth. Take a deep breath and as you exhale, slowly expand your hands as if inflating a balloon. When you are finished, take a deep breath and slowly close your hands back together as you inhale to 'deflate' the 'balloon'. Repeat this five times.

Simple yoga

These activities need a bit of floor space but are wonderfully calming:

- The Leaf – sit with spine straight, soles of feet together, hands on ankles. Gently round spine and then return to sitting straight. Repeat several times.

- The Flower – sit with spine straight, soles of feet together, hands on ankles. Gently bounce knees toward floor ten to twenty times.

Sticky hands

Ask the children to stand up and put their hands stiffly out in front of their bodies. Now show them how to press their hands together as if they are sticky hands and then push hard for twenty seconds. Tell the children to slowly allow their hands to come apart and see if they can feel the stickiness. Repeat this two or three times.

Simple stretches

Show the children how to do controlled, slow, stretches such as touching their toes then reaching up to the sky on their tip toes. If you have room, you can ask them to lie on their backs and make letters with their bodies. Try 'X' (spread out their legs and arms) and 'T', (put their legs together while keeping their arms stretched out). Be inventive and make up some more of your own as space allows. Show them how to move slowly from stretch to stretch.

Squeezes

Have the children form their hands into fists and bring their shoulders to their ears. Count to five with them and then relax. Repeat five times.

Gentle breathing

While they are sitting, ask the children to rest the tips of the fingers and thumbs of one hand against the fingers and thumbs of the other hand. Ask them to breathe slowly for one minute. This is very calming.

Massage

Show the children how to massage the sides of their eyes and temple with soothing fingers. Just move the fingers round and round in little circles. This is very relaxing.

Calming Visualisations

Visualisation techniques for children can help them relax and focus better during class; as well as developing their imagination and creativity. These calming visualisations are short and simple and perfect for restoring calm to an unsettled classroom. Before you start, make sure all the children are quiet and sitting comfortably in their chairs, with both feet slightly apart on the floor and their hands in their laps. Then read out the visualisation script in a clear, calm voice.

By the sea

We are going to close our eyes and imagine that we are by the sea. The beach is miles of soft, warm sand.

Think of the beach, it stretches as far as you can see. Imagine standing on the soft, white, warm sand. Feel your feet sinking into the softness. It feels so nice and comfortable.

Imagine that you are walking now, slowly. You lift one foot and place it down again; feeling it sink into the warm sand. Think of each step as you make it. Concentrate on the sand moving as you walk on it.

You look out to sea. It is the bluest blue you can imagine. You can see little glints of light where the sun reflects on the surface. Look at the water's edge, where the sea meets the sand. Gentle white waves break onto the shore. Imagine the sound of the waves. It is a gentle 'schlapp, schlapp' noise. It makes you feel drowsy.

Think of lying down on the warm sand. Imagine your body sinking into comfort. Feel the warmth and softness under your arms; imagine burying your hands into the sand, then lifting them out and watching the sand grains trickle off.

You look into the blue sky. Small white clouds drift across. They look like cotton wool; they are so fluffy. You can see birds flying high up; swooping and flying, graceful and quiet. You feel so peaceful and relaxed; it's such a nice place to be.

Enjoy the feeling for a little while longer and then slowly make your way back to the classroom. Open your eyes when you are ready and smile at the person next to you. Hold on to the good, calm feeling that your imagination has given you.

A secret place

We are going to close our eyes and imagine a special secret place that belongs just to you. Each person is going to have his or her own place which is the safest place in the world.

Imagine what your safe place will be like. Perhaps it is by the sea, or in a cave, or a special room. Imagine looking around your own special place – does it have any furniture in it? If it does, look at the furniture closely. Imagine the shape of your furniture; think of the colours of each piece. Imagine touching each item, stroking it, patting it, feeling that it all belongs just to you.

What can you see around your own special, safe place? What is the scenery like? Everything about your place is comfortable and familiar.

What sounds can you hear – birds singing, water? Anything else? The sounds are all nice, peaceful noises that you like to hear.

You love your safe place because you know that you can always go there whenever you are sad, angry or frightened and, because it is so perfect, you will soon feel better. Imagine how happy and contented you feel, being in your secret place, with all your favourite things around you. You feel that it is the best place in the whole world.

Now it is time to come back to the classroom. Take your time. Breathe deeply. Begin to notice the sounds around you and when you are ready open your eyes and smile at the person next to you. Hold on to the good, calm feeling that your imagination has given you.

The magical land

We are going to close our eyes and imagine that we are going on a journey to a magical land. A big silver spaceship has come to collect us. We are all sitting inside. It is ready to take off.

Imagine the spaceship has now started and is going faster and faster. Look out of your window and see the scenery whizzing by. Feel the speed of your spaceship; it is moving faster than you have ever been in your life before. Watch everything flashing by.

Now we have arrived at Rainbow Land. The spaceship stops and you walk off.

You look around you at the strange trees and flowers. Imagine trees with blue trunks and pink leaves, orange trunks and purple leaves, red trunks and yellow leaves. You are amazed at all the bright colours.

You can see beautiful butterflies and birds. Imagine what they look like; all different colours. Small furry animals come to greet you. They are friendly and rub up against your legs. They too are brightly coloured, with spots and stripes. Imagine what they look like. You bend down to stroke them, then pick them up and put your face on their soft silky fur. It smells nice. You breathe in the sweet pleasant smell and enjoy the feel of their warm furry bodies.

You look around at the houses. They are all brightly coloured as well. Notice all the different colours. Imagine a house that you would choose to live in. What is it like outside?

Imagine going into the house. What is the living room like? Think of all the furniture you would have in it. Now think of the bedroom. Think of all the nice things you would have in the bedroom. Imagine lying on the soft, comfortable bed. You feel relaxed and happy because you are in such a wonderful land.

Now it is time to come back to the classroom. Take your time. Breathe deeply. Begin to notice the sounds around you and when you are ready open your eyes and smile at the person next to you. Hold on to the good, calm feeling that your imagination has given you.

Calming the Senses

Children can experience a sense of disorientation, agitation and distraction when their senses are overloaded. They can lose their train of thought and find it impossible to concentrate, which can result in a very unsettled classroom. In this chapter you will find some useful tips on how you can use sensory experience to create a peaceful and composed setting in which purposeful work can resume.

Music in the classroom

Music has many uses in the classroom. If you select carefully it can be used to calm and relax children while they work. It can also be used to remove the distraction of 'white noise'. Classical music, in particular, stimulates alpha waves in the brain. The 'alpha state' can be described as 'relaxed alertness', when new information becomes much easier to absorb and memory is working at optimum power – just the state of mind you want to encourage in your classroom!

The best way to use music is to ask the children to relax and make themselves comfortable. Then suitable music is played at a level that is barely audible. Thus a calm ambience is achieved, alpha waves are stimulated and you can speak with a calm, quiet voice and the children can work on whatever task you set them.

These are some examples of alpha wave-producing music:

The Four Seasons	*Vivaldi*
The Music for the Royal Fireworks	*Handel*
Violin concertos 1 & 2	*Mendelssohn*
Tubular Bells	*Oldfield*
Symphony No. 3	*Glass*
The Quest	*Walton*
Canon	*Pachelbel*

A focused moment.

This activity helps children to learn that concentrating on their senses (rather than their emotions and thoughts) is very soothing. Ask them to sit very still and concentrate on the little details that are usually ignored. What can they hear? What can they feel on their skin – clothes, a slight breeze etc? Can they smell anything? Don't ask for answers, just let them sit and enjoy the state of being with their senses for a little while.

Calm-down bottles

Calm down bottles (see below) work well with many children. The child needs to shake the bottle, which offers a release to pent-up anger and anxiety. Then the child holds the bottle and watches the glitter slowly glide to the bottom. This stills the hands and body and focuses attention. The child's heartbeat slows and breathing steadies. Thus the falling glitter serves as a visual aid for the calming down that the child is experiencing.

Calm down bottles are easy to make. All you need is a sturdy plastic bottle with its label removed, clear gel tacky glue, some glitter, warm water and super glue. Mix all the ingredients except for the super glue in a jug. Pour the mixture into the bottle and seal the top with super glue.

About Jenny Mosley

Jenny Mosley is the author and founder of The Quality Circle Time Model and is well known nationally and internationally for her inspirational talks and motivational workshops.

Jenny's books and resources have received wide acclaim and Jenny Mosley Consultancies has an extraordinarily talented, highly experienced and well-supervised team of consultants who, along with Jenny, take the 'Quality Circle Time' model to the full range of educational settings: mainstream primary and secondary, independent and special schools, care homes and adult education.

Jenny's publishing company, Positive Press, has created a comprehensive catalogue of educational resources for use in early years settings and schools.

Resources for calmer classrooms

The Big Book of Calmers by Jenny Mosley & Ross Grogan

Better Behaviour Through Golden Time by Jenny Mosley

Jenny Mosley's Small Book Of The Golden Rules in Action

The Golden Rules Story Books by Donna Luck and Juliet Doyle

All resources can be ordered through Positive Press shop on the website **www.circle-time.co.uk** or phone **01225 719204** for a full catalogue.

For more information about training and resources:

Call: **01225 767157**
Email: **circletime@jennymosley.co.uk**
Website: **www.circle-time.co.uk**